Sarah Fuhrken

Revision. Key Moments in the Linguistic History of the English Speaking World

Prüfungsvorbereitung: Universität Bremen

GRIN Verlag

Bibliografische Information der Deutschen Nationalbibliothek:

Die Deutsche Bibliothek verzeichnet diese Publikation in der Deutschen National-
bibliografie; detaillierte bibliografische Daten sind im Internet über http://dnb.d-
nb.de/ abrufbar.

Imprint:

Copyright © 2014 GRIN Verlag GmbH
Druck und Bindung: Books on Demand GmbH, Norderstedt Germany
ISBN: 978-3-656-73400-0

This book at GRIN:

http://www.grin.com/en/e-book/279663/revision-key-moments-in-the-linguistic-
history-of-the-english-speaking

GRIN - Your knowledge has value

Der GRIN Verlag publiziert seit 1998 wissenschaftliche Arbeiten von Studenten, Hochschullehrern und anderen Akademikern als eBook und gedrucktes Buch. Die Verlagswebsite www.grin.com ist die ideale Plattform zur Veröffentlichung von Hausarbeiten, Abschlussarbeiten, wissenschaftlichen Aufsätzen, Dissertationen und Fachbüchern.

Visit us on the internet:

http://www.grin.com/

http://www.facebook.com/grincom

http://www.twitter.com/grin_com

Key Moments – Revision

1. Old English

History:
- lasted from **450-1100**
- **449:** Saxons, Jutes and Angles invaded England
- **heptarchy:** seven kingdoms:
  - Northumbria
  - Mercia
  - East Anglia
  - Kent
  - Essex
  - Sussex
  - Wessex
- Celts, Picts and Scots lived in England
- **8th century:** Vikings invaded East of England
- Danish king came on throne

Language:
- OE had **case inflexions** instead of prepositions; in **noun phrases**
- inflexion signals **case, gender, number**
- OE can have 1 of 3 word orders; 3 grammatical genders & 4 noun declensions
- vocabulary from native Germanic
- affixes, compounds and word-borrowings
- borrowed from Saxon, Latin, Jutes, Old Norse, Celtic
- OE is a **synthetic language:** dependent on inflection
- **analytic language:** dependent on word order

2. Middle English

History:
- **1100-1300:** Early Middle English
- **1300-1500:** Late Middle English (loss of case marking & inflexions)
- **1042:** King Edward the Confessor brought **French** to England
- **January 1066:** Edward died without child to follow him
- Harold, Earl of Wessex & Edward's second cousin William of Normandy battled
- **September 1066:** battle for throne: Harold was killed, William became king
- **1204:** struggle for Normandy → sense of English identity
- **1337-1453:** Hundred years war between England and France
- **1348: Black Death** 1/3 of population died; jobs became available on all levels; lower class people climbed social ladder; thus English climbed social ladder

Language:
- **French** became language of **court** & the **ruling class**
- **Latin** became language of **church** & **administration**
- lots of bilingual children
- word-borrowing from French
- English went from being a synthetic language to an analytic language
- instead of inflexions, the word order now signaled grammar case

3. Early Modern English

1500-1800
Translation of the Bible:
- Bible had huge effect on English language when it was translated
- **1380-82:** John Wycliffe's later banned translation led to increase of literacy
- **1522:** German translation of bible by Martin Luther
- **1525:** William Tyndale's later banned translation
- **1611:** King James Bible (first authorized translation)
- English became language of religion

Standardisation:
- **1476:** William Caxton set up **printing press**
- a standard form of English was needed
- **1480:** English-French dictionary by Caxton
- **1604:** first monolingual dictionary by Richard Cawdrey
- **1755:** Samuel Johnson's dictionary (43 000 words)

The Great Vowel Shift (1400-1650)
- vowel which is higher up in vowel chart was used instead of vowel below
- **position of tongue was raised**
- **push chain:** one vowel pushes the other away
- **drag chain:** other vowels are dragged in leftover spot
- → all vowels needed to be raised
- [i:] and [u:] were the highest and couldn't move any higher → turned into **diphthongs** [ti:d] & [hu:s] → [təid] & [həus] (not finished shift)

4. Inner, Outer and Expanding Circles

The two Diasporas of English:
- **1. Diaspora:** migrations to North America, Australia, New Zealand, South Africa
- **2. Diaspora:** colonization of Asia and Africa

The 3-way categorization:
- **ENL:** English as a native language
  - language of those born and raised in a country where English is historically the first language to be spoken
  - UK, USA, Canada, Australia, New Zealand
  - approx. 350 million speakers
- **ESL:** English as a second language
  - language spoken in once English territories
  - example: India, Nigeria, Singapore
  - approx. 350 million speakers
- **EFL:** English as a foreign language
  - language serves no purpose within the country
  - approx. 1 billion speakers with **reasonable competence**
- **ELF:** English as a **lingua franca** (spoken if no other language in common)
- **Difficulties with categorization:**
  - ENL is not a single variety of English
  - Pidgins & Creoles don't fit into categorization
  - large groups of ENL speakers in ESL territories and vice versa
  - quality of ENL language not considered

3 Circle Model (Kachru)
- most useful & influential model
- **Inner Circle** (ENL): first Diaspora
- **Outer Circle** (ESL): second Diaspora
- **Expanding Circle** (EFL)
- Problems:
    o population size out of date
    o placing for some countries not appropriate anymore
    o based on geography and history (proficiency not considered)
    o grey area in between circles

Centripetal Circles (Mondiano)
- **Proficiency in international English:** good cross-cultural communication; no strong dialect
- **Native/foreign language proficiency:** strong dialect
- **Learners:**
    o **interlanguage:** learner language which still improves
    o **fossilized language:** learners get stuck
- **Non-speakers**
- Problems:
    o Where to draw line between strong & non-strong accent?
    o What is international English?
    o How to measure proficiency?

Innovation, Deviation or Mistake?
- **Innovation:** creativity, often only ENL speakers (enjoyable)
- **Deviation:** other variety: "everyone has car" vs. "everyone has a car"
- **Mistake:** error

5. Pidgins and Creoles

Three types of English colony
- substantial settlements displaced pre-colonial population (1. Diaspora) (ex: North America; Australia)
- sparser colonial settlements; some of the natives learned ESL (2. Diaspora) (ex: Nigeria)
- pre-colonial population replaced by new labor from elsewhere (West Africa) (ex: Caribbean Islands of Barbados & Jamaica)

How did Pidgins & Creoles evolve?
- result of colonization; was used as a lingua franca
- **pidgin:** language with no native speakers; no one's first language but rather a contact language
- **creole:** defined as a pidgin that has become the first language of a new generation of speakers
- pidgin language: European + African/Asian language; fulfills restricted needs for people without a common language
- **Creolisation:** development of pidgin into creole; vocabulary expands & grammar gets more complex
    o **A:** Children of pidgin speaker use their parents pidgin as mother tongue
    o **B:** Pidgin used as lingua franca in multilingual areas; has more functions
- words are drawn from lexifier language (usually European)

- grammar is taken from indigenous language
- **reduplication** is used to:
  - intensify meaning (tok → tok tok)
  - avoid confusion (sip = ship; sip sip = sheep)

- **Pronunciation:**
  - fewer sounds
  - simplification of consonant clusters (col, frien instead of cold, friend)
  - conflation of consonant sounds (/f/, /p/ → pinis (finish))
- **Grammar:**
  - few inflections (no case-, gender-, tense-marking)
  - simple negative participle
  - no embedded clauses
  - one plural marker (the ten book)
- **Assimilation:** phonological process; speech sound changes & becomes more similar to another sound (/n/, /m/)
- **Reduction:** unstressed vowel that is pronounced with lax quality (the schwa)

6. North American English

- differs in spelling:
  - BE –our → AE –or (colour – color)
  - BE –ise → AE –ize (analyse – analyze)
  - BE –c → AE –s (defence – defense)
- differs in pronunciation ([r] rhotic and non-rhotic (car, tower))
- **dialect:** variation in pronunciation, vocabulary & grammar
- **accent:** pronunciation (regional or social)
- **isogloss:** line between dialects; measurable per feature
- **dialect boundary:** a few isoglosses come together
- **NORMS:** ideal informants for a questionnaire:
  - **N:** non-mobile
  - **O:** older
  - **R:** rural
  - **MS:** male speaker (females adapt to changes quicker)
- **sociolect:** depends on social background

7. Indian English

- around 1600: **East India Company** established
- **1947:** independence from Britain
- English for instructions, administration, legal system, parliament
- most books published in English
- India is 3rd largest English-using nation
- **Phonology:**
  - dental fricatives /θ/ and /ð/ noon-existent
  - tendency towards H-dropping (heat [i:t])
- **Prosodic features:** primary stress on penultimate syllable [tɜnˈdɜnsɪ]
- **Null-subjects/-objects: Pronoun-Drop** (pro-drop)
  - pro-drop allowed in vernacular IndE (variety)
  - allowed for pronouns in subject & object positions
  - "Take a dollar bill and insert [pro] in the machine"

8. English in the Southern Hemisphere _all are non-rhotic_

	Australian Englisch	New Zealand Englisch	Black South African English	White South African English
History	- Immigration of English people - accepting of local Aborigines language	- NZ colonized by British from different parts of GB→ different dialects - contact between natives & settlers: English language changed constantly	- colonization and slavery - Apartheid ended in 1994 → new lifestyle, diversity	- 1652: Dutch colonized Cape Town, 1795-1806: British conquest of the Dutch colony - development of two distinctive types of White South African
Phonology	- non-rhotic, regional, homogenous - long vowels are shortened; back vowels move to the front - use of final rising tone in declarative sentences	- speakers change [e] into [ɪ] in pronunciation. "Accent" → "accint". - change the [a] into [ɛ:] "The cat sat on a mat" → "The cet set on a met." - Words such as "bitter" with "th" instead of "tt".	- no lax/tense contrast - diphthongs often realized as monophthongs - in some cases consonants are simplified	- same words are used but meanings have changed (such as AmerE/BritE) - vocabulary expanded through borrowing (compounds and derivation)
Grammar	- Australian English speakers use "will" more often than "shall"	- noun morphology: s-genitive: animate creatures like human beings and animals of-genitive: things and abstract entities - avoidance of "shall"; instead "will" is used	- double conjunctions - can be able (not is able) - s in past tense (starts) - other are for this, other for that (some are for this....)	- tendency for voiceless plosives to be unaspirated in stressed word-inital
Lexis	- word borrowing from Aboriginal languages - loan translations: each morpheme of a word is translated into English - word formation using native English elements -ex.: baby carriage, stroller (AME) –Strollers (AUSE)	- words were leaned from AmE, BE and Maori AmE versions often commercially, BE versions used in everyday life. - Words: "yooroo" = goodbye "G'day" / "gidday" = Good day	- borrowed words from Dutch, BE and African English - borrowed words from slaves: Indonesia and Malaysia - reduplication and falling pitch	- deletion of verbal complements: the complements of transitive and ditransitive verbs may be omitted/ ellipsed _Did you bring?_

9. Language and Educational Policies

8 stages of language death (Fishman)
1. language exists in government, universities, media
2. used in local government & local mass media
3. used at work
4. used in school
5. local literacy in the community
6. children learn language from parents & community
7. cultural events & ceremonies
8. spoken by few isolated people

Are native speakers better teachers than non-natives?

Arguments for native speakers	Arguments for non-native speakers
• high proficiency • speak fluently • know more vocabulary • natural feeling for language • students feel more comfortable	• can explain differences in language better • learned the grammar rules • no dialect/colloquial language • may speak leaner's language • aware of problems of learners • interest in the language